CAN I TELL YOU ABOUT SELF-HARM?

CAN I TELL YOU ABOUT...?

The 'Can I tell you about...?' series offers simple introductions to a range of limiting conditions and other issues that affect our lives. Friendly characters invite readers to learn about their experiences, the challenges they face, and how they would like to be helped and supported. These books serve as excellent starting points for family and classroom discussions.

Other subjects covered in the Can I tell you about...? series

ADHD

Adoption

Anxiety

Asperger Syndrome

Asthma

Autism

Cerebral Palsy

Dementia

Depression

Diabetes (Type 1)

Down Syndrome

Dyslexia

Dyspraxia

Eating Disorders

Eczema

Epilepsy

Gender Diversity

ME/Chronic Fatigue
 Syndrome

Multiple Sclerosis

OCD

Parkinson's Disease

Pathological Demand
 Avoidance Syndrome

Peanut Allergy

Selective Mutism

Sensory Processing
 Difficulties

Stammering/Stuttering

Stroke

Tourette Syndrome

CAN I TELL YOU ABOUT
SELF-HARM?
A Guide for Friends, Family and Professionals

POOKY KNIGHTSMITH
Foreword by Jonathan Singer
Illustrated by Elise Evans

Jessica Kingsley *Publishers*
London and Philadelphia

First published in 2018
by Jessica Kingsley Publishers
73 Collier Street
London N1 9BE, UK
and
400 Market Street, Suite 400
Philadelphia, PA 19106, USA

www.jkp.com

Copyright © Pooky Knightsmith 2018
Foreword copyright © Jonathan Singer 2018
Illustrations copyright © Elise Evans 2018

Library of Congress Cataloging in Publication Data
A CIP catalog record for this book is available
from the Library of Congress

British Library Cataloguing in Publication Data
A CIP catalogue record for this book is
available from the British Library

ISBN 978 1 78592 428 6
eISBN 978 1 78450 796 1

Printed and bound in the United States

The text has been proofed in American English and
internationalized terminology has been used throughout to ensure
applicability to UK, US, Canadian and Australian readers.

To Clare, Mark and Rachel for giving me
the perfect balance of freedom and support
I need to help both myself and others.

CONTENTS

FOREWORD

I've been telling my three kids the same
bedtime story for years. One night my daughter
wouldn't go to sleep. The usual books and
songs weren't working. I was exhausted and
couldn't deal with another meltdown. So, in
a moment of desperation, I riffed on a story
I'd heard somewhere. It went something like
this: three little girls (whom I called Molly,
Rose and Ethan) were walking home from
school. There was a boulder in the road. They
moved it. Under the boulder was a pot of gold.
A leprechaun appeared and said that they
could keep the pot of gold because dozens of
people had passed and cursed the boulder,
but none had actually moved it. The sisters

were rewarded for their acts of kindness and justice. The girls were poor and now they were rich. The end. My daughter was delighted. Happy ending. Sleeping kid. I've made up hundreds of stories about the adventures of these three girls because they work. At the end of every story my kids are happy to go to sleep. And as any parent will tell you, that moment at the end of a long day when your child falls asleep is a blissful moment.

The thing about finding something that works is that even if you have loads of reasons why you should stop, it can be really hard to stop. Would it be better for my kids to fall asleep on their own? Probably. Should I be telling them increasingly fantastical stories about three rich girls who can do whatever they want? Probably not. But when I'm tired and can't handle the emotional overwhelm of tired screaming kids, I do what works. We all do.

The thing about self-harm is that it works: it distracts, it releases, it hides. For some, self-harm keeps away thoughts of suicide. You might have hurt yourself on impulse one day because things were so intense that you had to do something to make it stop. You didn't think you would do it again. But you did. And now, even though you can think of loads of reasons why you shouldn't, it is something you do because it works. It deals with that situation like nothing else.

But here's the other thing about self-harm: it doesn't work in the long run. There is a lot of research that says that youth who engage in non-suicidal self-injury over a long period of time are at higher risk for suicide (Whitlock *et al.*, 2013)[1]. Youth who self-injure and who report depression and substance abuse are at particular risk for suicide attempt (Jenkins, Singer, Conner, *et al.*, 2014)[2]. I'm not sharing this information to scare you. The fact that you're reading this book probably means you don't need to be scared. You probably want to stop, or you want to help someone who is self-harming. This book will help. Pooky has great insight into the *who, what, why, when* and *how* of self-harm. She presents it with compassion and without judgement.

---

1   Whitlock, J., Muehlenkamp, J. J., Eckenrode, J., Purington, A., Baral Abrams, G., Barreira, P., and Kress, V. (2013). Nonsuicidal self-injury as a gateway to suicide in young adults. *Journal of Adolescent Health*, 52(4), 486–492. https://doi.org/10.1016/j.jadohealth.2012.09.010

2   Jenkins, A. L., Singer, J. B., Conner, B. T., Calhoun, S., and Diamond, G. (2014). Risk for suicidal ideation and attempt among a primary care sample of adolescents engaging in nonsuicidal self-injury. *Suicide and Life-Threatening Behavior*, n/a-n/a. https://doi.org/10.1111/sltb.12094

I'm sure there will come a time when my kids won't ask for a "Molly, Rose and Ethan" story. I'm sure there will come a time when they age out of the sleep-inducing adventures of these three girls (just as most kids age out of self-harm behavior). But since they are 5 and 9, it won't be for several years. What I do know is that Pooky's book will help you long before that. Instead of years, you'll get the information you need to make changes in a matter of days. Pooky spells out why and how you can create a safety plan, get support and manage those overwhelming feelings. She acknowledges that overcoming self-harming behaviors will be easier some days and harder others. If you're ready to take that first step, this book is an excellent start. For those of you who are already on your way, this book is a great companion on your journey. Finally, if someone you love is self-harming, and you want to understand why and what you can do, this book is for you.

JONATHAN SINGER

Jonathan B. Singer is a clinical social worker, researcher and associate professor of social work at Loyola University Chicago. He has dedicated his 20-year career to working with families in crisis. He has 50 publications, including the co-authored book *Suicide in Schools*. He is the founder and host of the award-winning podcast series, the Social Work Podcast.

"Hi, my name is Asher and I'm 14. I'm pretty much like most regular 14-year-olds, I play in the school hockey team and like to hang around with my friends, listen to music and spend way too much time on social media if my mum is to be believed. I live at home with my mum and my dog, Buddy. One thing that makes me a bit different from some of my friends is that, when things feel too much for me, I sometimes hurt myself to manage how I'm feeling."

"It's kind of hard to describe self-harm because it can refer to a really wide range of behaviors. I mostly self-harm by cutting or scratching myself, but my friend Annalee sometimes takes medicines or eats or drinks things that she shouldn't – sometimes poisonous chemicals and things like that. Then there's our friend Mikey who punches walls and doors when he gets angry and Nina who doesn't exactly do anything to hurt herself, but neither does she do the things she needs to look after herself, like eating or sleeping properly or taking care when she crosses the road. Not realizing that there are lots of different ways of self-harming can stop people asking for help when they need it because they don't realize that they're self-harming or that there's anything that can be done to help. It's also important that we don't tell our friends too many details about the specific ways in which we harm ourselves since it might put ideas into people's heads about ways they might hurt themselves too."

"Self-harm can affect anyone of any age, any gender, any ethnicity, any anything! Self-harm is a lot more common than it used to be and people are doing it at younger ages than before. Most people think that self-harm is something that only affects teenage girls, but that's not true.

Some people self-harm once or twice but then they don't do it again either because the problem they were struggling with gets better or because self-harm didn't help them to feel better. Other people might carry on struggling with self-harm for weeks or months or even years. Some people will do it occasionally; others do it several times a day."

"Some people think self-harm is just a way of attention seeking.

Instead of dismissing someone who harms themselves as an attention seeker, it is more helpful to stop and ask yourself, 'Why might they need some support or attention?' or, 'How can I help?'

Some people harm themselves in secret, hiding their injuries or hurting themselves on parts of the body where it's not likely to be seen – this is definitely not attention seeking, in fact they might find it especially hard to ask for help at all."

"Some people share pictures of their injuries on social media and, once, when I was looking for support to help me stop self-harming, I came across some really toxic forums where people were actually encouraging each other to self-harm and sharing hints and tips and stuff.

They also showed pictures of their injuries and scars to see whose were the worst. It made me feel quite scared and luckily I didn't get sucked into it, but some people do, especially if they don't have anyone to talk to in real life who they feel understands them and their behavior.

Social media isn't always bad though, despite what people might think. Sometimes I find that it can be easier to ask for support online than to pick up the phone or talk to someone face to face. I take care never to share pictures or details of my own injuries though as I know these can be distressing for other people or encourage them to hurt themselves too, even if that wasn't my intention. As well as being able to talk to friends online, there are some good websites too – like the Young Minds website – www.youngminds.org – which has lots of information and advice to help you get better or to know how to help a friend. You have to be careful what information you access about self-harm online though; you always have to ask yourself who wrote this website and why. Usually websites run by health or education organizations or charities are the kinds of places you will find the most useful and safe information."

"Self-harm can feel so lonely. Until I opened up to people and gave them a chance to understand. I felt like no one understood, not my friends or my family or my teachers or even my doctor. My dog helped me feel a little less alone."

"There are loads of different reasons why people self-harm and if you know someone who is struggling with self-harm it's important that you don't make any assumptions about why they're doing it. If you feel comfortable doing so, talk to them about it and let them tell you their story, in their words. They might not even really understand it themselves yet, but talking about it can help them to understand it better and it can help them to feel less alone and help you to understand.

Everyone's story is different but here are some of the most common reasons people say they harm themselves:

ESCAPE

If life feels chaotic, stressful or otherwise difficult to manage, self-harm can feel like a way of escaping all of those worries for a little while.

RELEASE OF FEELINGS

Hurting yourself can help to release feelings – like you're an over inflated balloon and you're letting a little bit of air out before you pop.

PHYSICAL RATHER THAN EMOTIONAL PAIN

For some people, physical pain can be a way of communicating emotional pain, which is too hard to talk about. Or it can provide a more manageable form of pain that they can tend to rather than facing up to the emotional and psychological injuries they may be suffering with, for example, as a result of abuse.

PUNISHMENT

Some people hurt themselves as a way of punishing themselves when they don't live up to expectations – either because they set really high standards for themselves or because they've been punished a lot in the past and feel that they deserve to be punished (even though they don't).

NOWHERE ELSE TO TURN

Sometimes, people hurt themselves because they don't know of any better ways of managing their problems."

"I don't want to die and that's true for many people who struggle with self-harm. In a way self-harm is often more about wanting to stay alive; it's a way of trying to cope with life so you can make it from one hour to the next. A lot of people wrongly assume that if someone hurts themselves or takes an overdose of medication it means that they are suicidal – and whilst that is true for some people, it's not true for most. Again, the only way you can ever really know for sure is to have a conversation with the person you're concerned about.

People with a history of self-harm are more at risk of attempting suicide than people who have never harmed themselves. This is especially true if the experiences and feelings underlying the self-harming behaviors are not addressed and managed, which is one of the reasons why it's so important that people who self-harm are given the chance to talk through their issues and access further support if it's needed.

It's important that self-harm is taken seriously and that people like me receive support, caring and understanding because even though we might never have had any thoughts of suicide, self-harm is currently the strongest predictor the medical community has of later death by suicide – things can get better, or worse, over time.

Sometimes self-harm is the only way I can find of managing to get from one minute to the next. It doesn't mean I want to die; it's the best way I know of managing my feelings and staying alive right now. However, if things got worse instead of better then feelings of wanting to die might start to creep in."

"It can be very hard to stop self-harming, so it's important that people who regularly hurt themselves learn how to do so safely and are taught how to look after their injuries. Sadly, people can get really poorly as a result of infected wounds, or if they hurt themselves more seriously than they intended to.

I got really good advice from a nurse who told me about preventing infection by sterilizing the things I used to hurt myself with. She also taught me how to clean and dress my wounds. The other thing she told me was how to recognize if I was going into shock, which can happen if you hurt yourself badly or suddenly lose a lot of blood.

Going into shock can be dangerous as you might pass out and hit your head or something. The nurse told me if I thought I might be going into shock, I should find an adult I trusted and tell them what was happening. Feeling shaky, dizzy, sick, clammy or breathing really fast were the signs she told me to look out for. Luckily I've never had any infections or gone into shock, but I feel better knowing how to look after myself.

It's a good idea to get your wounds checked regularly; I go to see the nurse so she can check my injuries and make sure that I'm looking after them okay."

"If you know someone who self-harms then the first thing you'll probably want to do is to tell them to stop, but this can be terribly hard to do for two main reasons. First, because the self-harm is fulfilling a purpose – we are doing it for a reason, to make us feel better in some way and to cope with difficult feelings or experiences that we wouldn't know how to manage otherwise. Second, if we've been doing it for a while, it can be quite habit-forming, like biting your nails, and sometimes quite addictive too because it makes us feel a little bit better – which feels good. Asking someone to stop hurting themselves instantly can put unrealistic expectations on them. In order to be able to stop they need to develop healthy coping strategies to replace the current unhealthy self-harm behaviors. This won't happen overnight, so there is often a period whilst someone is trying to stop that they need to be supported in decreasing how often and how badly they hurt themselves, improve how safely they do it, and spend some time learning to understand themselves and what drives their behavior and finding alternative ways to cope."

"People are often really scared to talk about self-harm and friends, family members or professionals who work with a young person who is regularly hurting themselves can find it hard to know what to say or do. But the truth is that, often, it is the people who are involved in our day to day lives who can be the most help of all, simply by listening and trying to understand, and by supporting us when we are experiencing big feelings that might make us more likely to self-harm. Knowing that our friends, family members and people like our teachers know what's going on and that we can talk to them if we're struggling is a big help.

For some young people, it can be helpful to get some professional support from a counsellor or specialist of some kind. This is especially true if their self-harming behaviors are dangerous, if they have been going on a long time, if they are getting worse or if they need specialist help for the underlying reasons – if, for example, they are being abused. The other time we might need the help of a health professional or counsellor is if we have got other mental health problems. Sometimes, our injuries are the first thing people become aware of, but we might also be suffering with other illnesses we need help with, like depression, anxiety or an eating disorder.

I found it incredibly hard to talk to someone about my self-harm at first because I felt guilty, ashamed and embarrassed, but once I had started talking to people it made it a lot easier for me to stop. I would advise anyone who is struggling with self-harm to talk to an adult they trust, maybe a parent, a teacher or a doctor who can help them to get the support that they need to stay safe and learn new ways of coping. It helps so much to feel listened to and really heard – even if it's just for a few minutes."

66 **T**here is increasing evidence that talking
therapies like CBT (cognitive behavioral
therapy) and skills based therapies like DBT
(dialectical behavioral therapy) can help people
who self-harm, especially those over 18.

The best way to find out what treatment is
available is to ask your doctor or your school.

They will often want to learn more about
the person who is hurting themselves and
try to work out how much risk they are at
and whether they are suffering from another
illness which needs treatment, like depression,
anxiety or an eating disorder.

What treatment is available varies from
place to place and might include things like
online counselling, face to face counselling
or group-based support. In a perfect world,

everyone who needed help with their self-harm would quickly receive support from health professionals who've had specialist training, but, sadly, because so many of us self-harm and schools and doctors don't always have as much money as they need to help everybody, some people who harm themselves will not get specialist treatment at all, or they might need to wait for quite a long time. This can be especially difficult if friends and family find our behavior hard to understand and don't feel able to help.

There are sources of further information for friends, family or staff who are worried about a young person who is self-harming (see the Recommended Reading, Websites and Organizations at the end of this book).

Unfortunately, the waiting list for specialist help can be long. Where it is available, specialist support is usually between three and twelve sessions long and will normally involve a lot of talking and trying to understand what is making us feel the need to self-harm so that we can try and understand these issues and think about how to either change or manage the situation and our feelings. The sessions will also often be skills-based – that means that, as well as talking about self-harm, we get a chance to think about what practical things might help. We might learn skills about how to understand and manage our emotions to stop them building to the point where we need to self-harm and we might also learn a range of different ways of coping with these feelings in a healthy way instead of hurting ourselves. We might also learn to question the thoughts that lead us to self-harm. For example, if we think we deserve to be punished, a therapist might help us to question that thought and try to find evidence to back up whether it is right or wrong – if we can learn to question our thoughts this way, rather than assuming that the negative things we think about ourselves are true, then sometimes we might find that we don't feel the urge to self-harm so strongly. It takes time and practice though.

Many people who self-harm get better without specialist help and are able to overcome their self-harm through the care and support of friends, family and other trusted adults in their lives, like teachers or youth workers. However, any time someone injures themselves badly, or if they begin to think about killing themselves, they should be taken straight to the hospital or doctor. Also, if things are clearly getting worse rather than better, then it is worth going back to the doctor to ask for help again."

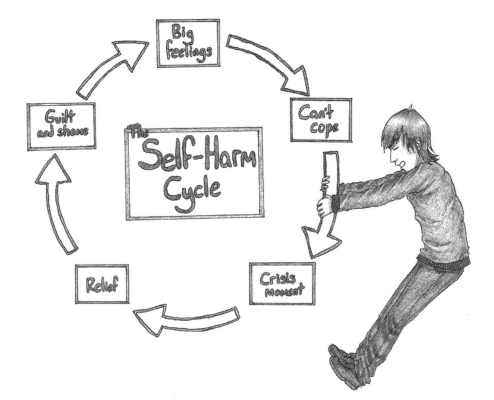

"When I first started hurting myself, I just did it occasionally but, over time, I found myself turning to it more and more as a means of coping with my feelings. It can quickly become a cycle that is hard to break.

For me, the cycle of self-harm would start with my head getting filled with big feelings of guilt and shame; I didn't know any healthy ways of managing those feelings so I'd end up feeling totally unable to cope. I'd be like a pan of milk sitting on the hob, I'd be simmering away until suddenly it became too much and my feelings would suddenly boil over, just like hot milk. That boiling over is a crisis moment and that's when I'd hurt myself.

For a little while I would feel better, I'd get a sense of relief – but it never lasted long. As my feelings died down and I was faced with what I'd done to myself, again, I'd feel a mix of different feelings like regret, guilt and shame. I'd think about how I was letting everyone down and how other people seemed much more able to manage their feelings, so why couldn't I? These thoughts and feelings would pile on top of the original feelings – so, in fact, hurting myself made things worse not better – but I still didn't have another way of coping and so I'd end up hurting myself again, because it was the only way I knew how to feel better for a little while.

With the help of my counsellor, I learned that to break the cycle, I needed to make changes to my life that meant that I didn't experience the feelings that drove me to self-harm. That was possible with some things – for example I stopped using some social media apps I was getting bullied on. But it was harder with other things – homework still had to be done and exams came around. My counsellor taught me that I could also break the cycle by changing the way I coped – so instead of hurting myself, which is an unhealthy coping mechanism, I gradually learned new healthier ways of coping. Finally, I'm learning that by beginning to understand and manage my emotions better, I don't so often reach crisis point, so I'm hurting myself less often – my milk pan doesn't boil over as much!"

"What works is different for everyone so it's not exactly a case of one size fits all – and sometimes I find that something that didn't work at all a few days ago works well now, so you have to be flexible and try new things.

We need to create a whole toolbox of different ways of coping we can call on at different times.

The sorts of alternatives that can work instead of turning to self-harm will depend on the reason someone is hurting themselves. If I can take a minute and ask myself, 'Why would self-harm make me feel better right now?' then I am halfway to working out a healthier alternative.

Here are some examples:

Things that help if I feel angry and I need to feel calmer:

- Listening to calming music

- Doing a few minutes of mindfulness or meditation

- Blowing bubbles

- Taking ten deep breaths

- Sitting outside and counting all the different things I can see, smell or hear.

Things that help if I feel like I should be punished:

- Ask myself if I really deserve to be punished; what would I say to a friend in the same situation?

- Think about what I have done that deserves punishing and make a plan to do things differently next time

- Write the bad things I am thinking on my skin instead of hurting myself

- Scream (either out loud or in my head).

It can be hard to think up alternatives when we're in crisis mode, so a helpful thing to do, if possible with a friend or supportive adult, is to brainstorm ideas and practise doing them at times when we feel calm. That makes it a lot easier to remember to try them when things feel too much. I also found that keeping a note of my alternatives in my phone or on a card in my wallet helped me as I could remind myself when I wasn't thinking straight."

"The other thing that I've learned about self-harm is that those crisis moments, when it feels like hurting myself is the only thing in the world that will help, only actually last for quite a short amount of time. It's like my body is screaming and screaming and needs a valve released, but if I can just stick with it for a few minutes then the screaming gets quieter and eventually I start to feel calmer again. It's really hard to just sit there whilst your body and your brain are screaming though so it's good to have a range of things to try and distract you. Things I've found useful include:

- A countdown timer – either on my phone or an egg timer – I see if I can manage one minute without hurting myself, then two, then three...

- A playlist of songs that make me feel better. I challenge myself to get to the end of a song without hurting myself. If I manage song one, can I do song two?

- Physical activity – stuff like seeing if I can do 100 jumping jacks – that also has the added benefit of helping to work some of my anxiety out of my system.

- I find talking to people helpful, or having them talk to me. They don't necessarily need to know that I'm trying not to self-harm unless I feel comfortable telling them. Sometimes when I most need help it's the middle of the night, but even then there is someone you can talk to by phoning or texting people like The Samaritans or ChildLine.

Sometimes alternatives and distractions work, sometimes they don't. That's okay but I do feel proud every time I manage to avoid hurting myself and it really helps me if my friends, family or adults who are supporting me can help me to focus in on the times I succeed in not self-harming and looking at what we can learn from that, rather than getting upset about my new injuries which often makes me feel like I'm failing or letting down the people who care about me."

"I don't mind if people ask me about my injuries or scars, but some people do. For me, each of my injuries tells a story and sometimes it can be helpful to talk about it with the right person. It can also help to have an adult check that my injuries are healing okay and that they're not infected and stuff. I don't always have a lot to say though; I can get quite shy and embarrassed about it.

New injuries should be kept clean and covered to reduce the risk of infection, but when it comes to scars, it's a much bigger question. I've been told that I should dress for the weather – if that means wearing a short sleeve t-shirt and people seeing my scars then that's okay so long as I'm comfortable with it. I've also been told I should imagine they were accidental scars and make decisions about whether to cover them up or not, just as I would if I'd got them in a car accident.

That's all easier said than done though and I can't help but wonder what people are thinking about me if they see my scars.

Sometimes, when my scars aren't covered up, other people will confide in me about their self-harm so I always have to be ready for that. I sometimes also get questions or hurtful comments about them, so again, I have to be mentally prepared for that possibility. More often than not though, people say nothing at all – and sometimes that's the hardest thing of all because my scars and my self-harming behaviors have become quite a major part of who I am and how I identify myself; so when people don't even notice, that can feel kind of strange.

My scars are a part of my story and as I grow to accept them, and as they fade with time, I begin to feel less uncomfortable wearing clothes than don't cover them up."

66 The most important thing you can do is to carry on being my friend – do the same stuff with me that we used to do before you learnt about my self-harming. It can be really helpful if we can spend time talking about things that we're both finding difficult and thinking about safe, healthy ways to manage any difficult feelings we might have. It can also be helpful if you can remind me of some of my healthy ways of coping if you think things are becoming too hard for me.

Another important thing you can do as a friend is to help me to get the help and support I need from a trusted adult like a parent, teacher or doctor. This might feel like the last thing a friend should do and I might tell you about my self-harm and ask you not to tell anyone, but in the long-term I'll thank you –

in fact that's exactly what happened when I told my friend Simon. I begged him not to tell anyone but he didn't know how to help me on his own and he was really worried about me, so he told my mum.

I was really angry at first and even stopped talking to him for a little while, but after a while I realized it had been unfair of me to expect him not to tell anyone and I also realized he had done the right thing, because, whilst Simon was a good friend, he couldn't help as much as my mum or my doctor. If you have a friend who is hurting themselves, you could also suggest that you go with them to tell a parent, teacher or doctor together so they feel less alone. You can help them work out what to say and be there for moral support because it's a pretty tough conversation.

The most important thing a friend can do is just to keep being a friend. Just be normal. I'm still me!"

"The most important thing you can do is listen and let me talk. It might feel awkward and it might take a while. You're probably going to feel all sorts of different feelings like anger, sadness or even disgust or guilt. You might feel like this is your fault – but try to remember that this is about me, not about you. Take time to listen and try not to make any assumptions about why I'm doing it and please try not to judge or over-react. If you respond calmly and give me space to think and talk (even if you're screaming in your head!) then I am likely to feel like I can trust you and continue to talk to you about my self-harm as I begin to take steps to overcome it.

Try not to get angry if I can't stop straight away, and help me to feel proud of small successes instead of ashamed of the times when I can't overcome the urge to hurt myself. If in the past week there have been 19 times when the urge to hurt myself overcame me, and one time when I managed to avoid it, let's focus in on that one time and think about what went right and how we can learn from it.

I know it's hard, but please try to accept that this is my way of coping and managing and that it can change with your help and support, but only if I feel loved, accepted and able to take a little time and space to learn healthier ways of coping."

"There are loads of different things that the various professionals in our lives – teachers, support works and doctors, for example – can do. Like everyone else, the most important thing you can do is listen to me without assumption or judgement.

As a professional, you are often uniquely well placed to help me access specialist support. You might also act as the person who takes on an informal counselling role, listening to me regularly in-between sessions – or in place of them if there is a lack of services.

You can take practical steps to help me each day, by discussing my trigger points – I once had a great conversation with a teacher who asked me to tell her about a typical school day from the moment I woke up until the moment I went to bed. As I talked her through the day, we explored which points were most likely to distress me and result in me feeling the urge to hurt myself; then we thought together about which of those points were things we could address. Sometimes simple, highly practical suggestions can make a huge difference in helping me to turn things around. A homework extension, somewhere quiet to retreat to at break time and access to first aid supplies without a barrage of questions and judgement were all things that my teacher helped me put in place. Her help made me feel heard and understood. It also relieved some of the tangible pressures I was feeling at the time. It was the start of things beginning to get better.

Working with a trusted adult to think about how to manage day to day challenges can be helpful."

❝I've been hurting myself for a long time now, and it's going to take a while for me to stop. But with friends, family and professionals in my life who listen, who care and who help me to celebrate my small successes and look for practical ways to address upcoming stresses and challenges, I feel more able to manage and move forwards.

I will be left with permanent reminders of the times I hurt myself, in the shape of the physical scars that are left on my skin. But with time and acceptance from those I love, both now and in the future, I hope to learn to accept each of these scars as a symbol not of a time I failed, but of a time that I managed. I hope that you and I will both be able to look at my scars as they heal and then fade, and remember what remarkable courage and teamwork it took for me to overcome this – we've all got a part to play in this story, and together we can determine what the next chapter looks like.❞

"It's important to remember and acknowledge that no truth we can tell a child is likely to be as bad as the truth they may imagine if we leave them to fill in the blanks without adult guidance.

There are ten things that every child who has a sibling, parent or other loved one who is struggling with self-harm or a mental health issue needs to hear:

1. You are not alone.

2. You are loved unconditionally.

3. It's okay to ask questions.

4. There is nothing to be afraid of.

5. Things can get better.

6. It's not your fault.

7. Sometimes when people seem angry, it's because they're poorly.

8. It's okay to have fun and smile.

9. I am always happy to listen to you.

10. Never be afraid to ask for help.

In terms of explaining the injuries themselves, quite how honest you are depends on the relationship with the child and their age and stage of understanding. I have found a useful analogy to be chicken pox. Most kids have experienced chicken pox and they know that when they were poorly their body got covered in chicken pox blisters and scabs. As they got better, these started to heal. Some of the scars will never go away – most of us have one or two chicken pox scars we can share with our children."

FINAL THOUGHTS FROM POOKY

Thank you for taking the time to read this book. Whilst self-harm is on the increase amongst people of all ages, it's still a topic that many people feel deeply uncomfortable talking about or seeking help with. By reading this book and trying to understand a little better how you can help yourself or someone you care about, you are helping to break down the stigma and taboo that have historically surrounded self-harm.

If you, or someone you care about, are trying to overcome self-harming behaviors, please be forgiving. There will be good days and bad days and a slip or blip does not mean you're back at square one, no matter how it might feel. Progress is rarely linear.

If you still have questions about self-harm after reading this book then why not drop me a line? The very best way to reach me is via Twitter – @PookyH. I'll always do my best

to answer your questions, both as someone
who carries many scars and fights the urge to
self-harm every day and as someone who has
spent a long time researching and teaching and
learning about the topic.

Every day is a new beginning. Take a deep
breath and start again.

Good luck!

Pooky

Twitter: @PookyH
Instagram: @PookyH
Email: pooky@inourhands.com
Website: www.inourhands.com

RECOMMENDED READING, WEBSITES AND ORGANIZATIONS

BOOKS

Fitzpatrick, C. (2012) *A Short Introduction to Understanding and Supporting Children and Young People Who Self-Harm.* London: Jessica Kingsley Publishers.

Knightsmith, P. (2015) *Self-Harm and Eating Disorders in Schools: A Guide to Whole-School Strategies and Practical Support.* London: Jessica Kingsley Publishers.

Knightsmith, P. (2016) *The Healthy Coping Colouring Book and Journal: Creative Activities to Manage Stress, Anxiety and Other Big Feelings.* London: Jessica Kingsley Publishers.

RESOURCES

Healthtalk – www.healthtalk.org/peoples-experiences/mental-health/self-harm-parents-experiences/topics

No Harm Done – videos and information for young people, parents and professionals concerned about self-harm
www.inourhands.com/noharmdone

Coping with Self-Harm – A Guide for Parents and Carers – information booklet for parents developed by the Oxford University Department of Psychiatry – download or order free hard copies at www.cwmt.org.uk/resources

WEBSITES

www.cwmt.org.uk – mental health charity which provides free training and resources to support young people's emotional wellbeing and mental health

www.youngminds.org.uk – information for young people, parents and professionals about a wide range of mental health issues

www.inourhands.com – Pooky Knightsmith's website including webinars, podcasts, resources and blog posts about mental health

HELPLINES

The Samaritans
UK: 116 123

ChildLine
UK: 0800 1111
US: 1-800-422-4453
Canada: 1800 668 6868
Australia: 1800 55 1800